PIRATES
AND
SHIPWRECKS

TRUE STORIES

Real Tales of Terror on the High Seas

TOM McCARTHY

Current titles in the **Mystery & Mayhem** Series

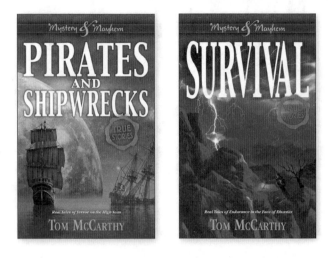

Check out more titles at www.nomadpress.net

Nomad Press
A division of Nomad Communications
10 9 8 7 6 5 4 3 2 1

This book was manufactured by CGB Printers,
North Mankato, Minnesota, United States
October 2016, Job #208074
ISBN Softcover: 978-1-61930-475-8
ISBN Hardcover: 978-1-61930-471-0

Educational Consultant, Marla Conn

Questions regarding the ordering of this book should be addressed to
Nomad Press
2456 Christian St.
White River Junction, VT 05001
www.nomadpress.net

Printed in the United States.

MIX
Paper from
responsible sources
FSC® C008080

Contents

Introduction
Terror on the High Seas

Arrrrrrgghh! Imagine you're asleep in a
swinging hammock on a creaking ship, miles
from any land, surrounded by people who
haven't had baths in weeks. Now, imagine that
a crack of lightning signals the start of a terrible
storm, a storm that will toss your ship high over
waves and deep into trouble. Do you survive
the storm? Do you find a raft and make it to
shore? What then? Who's there to greet you? Are
they friends or are they bloodthirsty pirates?

In this book, you won't find any boring stories
about people doing ordinary things in ordinary
places. Instead, you'll meet people who find
themselves in dire situations where the wrong
move could mean death or disaster.

Daniel Collins was a young man from Maine who was on his way to becoming a captain of his own ship. He had second thoughts about long cruises after his trip to Cuba was cut short by pirates—real pirates, not the storybook kind.

There's also Captain Francis Leopold McClintock, who was the perfect man to try to solve the mystery of Captain Sir John Franklin and his crew, who disappeared into the frozen landscape of the Arctic in 1845. Captain McClintock's main goal, beyond surviving the excruciating living conditions? To settle nasty rumors that Captain Franklin and his men suffered a fate worse than death.

In this book, you'll meet a woman who spent most of her life dressed as a man, and to great effect. Mary Read was known and feared as one of the fiercest pirates to ever sail the Caribbean— she was brave enough to outfight her own shipmates alongside her friend, Anne Bonny, another fearsome female pirate!

On some deserted islands, it's not pirates you have to be afraid of—it's cannibals! This is what Captain William Clement Doutty was concerned with when his ship ran aground on a tiny island near India, right next to another British ship that had weathered the same terrible storm. Will the two groups be able to keep from starving and from becoming a celebration dinner for the hostile islanders?

Then there is Barbarossa, a short, one-armed captain who frightened everyone, especially the fussy and prim crews of some of the royal ships he attacked and burned and plundered. From a childhood spent selling his father's pottery to becoming the most feared pirate in the Mediterranean, Barbarossa shows what motivation and cunning can do for a career on the high seas.

Ready to take a sea voyage?

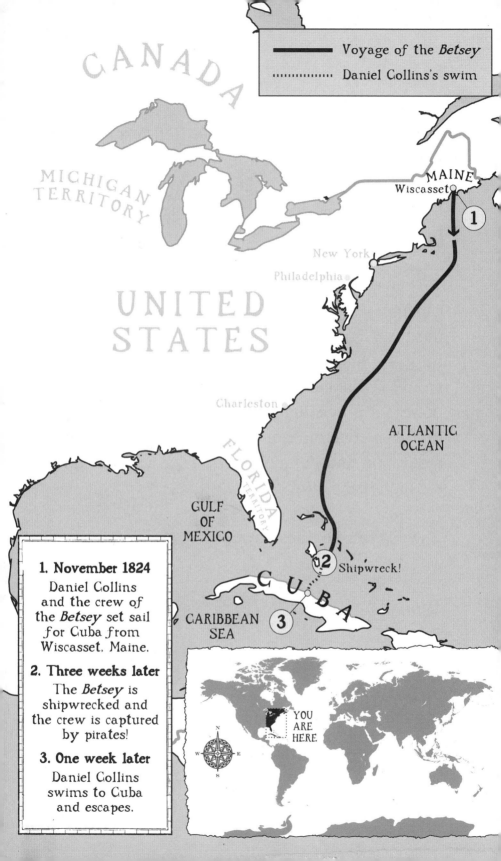

Voyage of the *Betsey*
.... Daniel Collins's swim

CANADA

MICHIGAN TERRITORY

MAINE
Wiscasset

①

New York
Philadelphia

UNITED STATES

Charleston

FLORIDA TERRITORY

ATLANTIC OCEAN

GULF OF MEXICO

C U B A

② Shipwreck!

CARIBBEAN SEA

③

1. November 1824
Daniel Collins and the crew of the *Betsey* set sail for Cuba from Wiscasset, Maine.

2. Three weeks later
The *Betsey* is shipwrecked and the crew is captured by pirates!

3. One week later
Daniel Collins swims to Cuba and escapes.

YOU ARE HERE

N
W · E
S

Chapter One

The Lucky Escape of Daniel Collins

A tale of desperate men, fierce pirates, and missing heads, adapted from the *Narrative of the Shipwreck of the Brig Betsey, of Wiscasset, Maine, and Murder of Five of Her Crew, By Pirates, on the Coast of Cuba, Dec. 1824*. It is by Daniel Collins, one of only two survivors.

Walk slowly into an old Maine graveyard today and you can still see the tombstones of the young men. They are farther back, behind neater rows of graves from more recent times. But you can find them if you look, and you can still make out the words carved into the granite markers almost two hundred years ago.

Hiram Walker　　　　　*Ebediah Pettingill*

1808–1826 Lost at Sea　　　*1818–1834 Missing at Sea*

In those days, young men went to sea and many did not come home. Unexpected storms, leaky ships, bad charts, and maybe just bad luck—it was a hard life to go to sea.

Daniel Collins was an ambitious, up-and-coming sailor, and he knew from the time he was a boy that he wanted to go to sea. He was already third mate of the *Betsey*, just two men away from being a captain, which was his goal.

In November 1824, the plan was to get some good Maine lumber—pine and birch from the nearby banks of the Sheepscot River—load it onto the *Betsey*, make the fairly safe trip down to Cuba, unload it, and come back home.

The seven-man crew didn't know that five of them would soon have their names carved into tombstones in graveyards around the small village of Wiscasset. They didn't know their bones would soon be scattered on the white, sandy beach of a small island called the Cross of the Father, not too far from Cuba.

We know where the bones are. But we don't know whether the heads of those young sailors are in the same place.

Things began to go wrong very quickly on the way down to Cuba. The captain, Ellis Hilton, an experienced and kind man who had made the trip to Cuba before, was sick almost the whole way. He spent a lot of time in his bunk in his cabin. That made the mood on board a bit tense. Crews need leadership to give them confidence.

Three weeks after they left Wiscasset, Maine, the *Betsey* made it to the warm and shallow waters of the Caribbean Sea, a place dotted with islands. Some of the islands were regular stops for boats from Maine. Other islands meant danger, with rocks and hidden underwater reefs lying in wait to trap sailors who didn't know where they were going or were tired and a little careless. Maybe they had a sick captain who couldn't give directions.

The captain ordered that the *Betsey* anchor and the crew take a well-deserved rest near a beautiful, unknown island. That would be the last rest all of them would take.

That night, Daniel Collins had an unsettling dream.

The dream frightened him so much he couldn't get back to sleep. He bolted upright in his bunk, worried, but not sure why. The dream put him on edge. In a very short time, that uneasiness would save his life.

The next day, they pulled up anchor. They were almost to Cuba and the captain was anxious to deliver the lumber and be paid. That night, the wind picked up, becoming stronger and more unpredictable. Captain Hilton, who had been in his cabin as usual, came out briefly to take a look.

When Daniel Collins saw the captain emerge from his cabin, he asked if he could drop some of the sails to slow the boat down and make things a bit safer. He worried about a storm.

Captain Hilton said no. Time was money, and there was no time to slow down now that they were so close to dropping off the cargo. When the captain went back to his cabin, Daniel Collins took charge as the night became so dark and starless he could barely see his hand in front of his face.

Later that night, when the first mate, Joshua Merry, came up to take over steering, Daniel Collins told him, "All is well."

Daniel Collins went to his bunk, but couldn't sleep. A half hour later, any chance of nodding off ended quickly and violently when the *Betsey* hit something very hard and unforgiving. There was a tremendous crashing explosion of noise. Daniel Collins was thrown from his bunk and covered with boxes and barrels from storage.

The *Betsey* had hit an underwater reef and was sinking. Her thick wooden sides had ripped open and water was rushing in.

The *Betsey*'s wide and solid bow had been torn off like a thin piece of tissue paper. The boat came apart quickly, groaning and screaming, as if it were alive.

The valuable cargo the crew had loaded three weeks before rushed out to sea, lost forever. The crew leaped from the crumbling ship, then pulled themselves into the *Betsey's* one lifeboat, which had come loose and floated nearby.

Then they watched, stunned, as the *Betsey* sank to the bottom.

Daniel Collins was happy to see the captain's dog had made it into the lifeboat. Not for sentimental reasons, though. If they couldn't reach the safety of land, the dog would make a nice dinner, he thought.

At least they were all alive—Captain Hilton, Joshua Merry, Daniel Collins, Charles Manuel, Seth Russel, Benjamin Bridge, and the cook, Detrey Jerome. But things had changed. There would be no delivering lumber to Cuba, no Christmas celebrations, and no warm sunshine on the beach while they counted their hard-earned money.

That was not even the worst of it. But, of course, they didn't know that at the time.

The lifeboat leaked. It leaked so badly that the soaked and frightened survivors who weren't busy rowing had to move in a frenzy to bail out the water that was rushing in. They only had one bucket and two canvas hats. This was not an efficient way to remove hundreds of gallons of water from the boat!

As the waves grew larger and the winds blew harder, the sailors did what sailors always do— they improvised. They made a flimsy sail from a ship's blanket they found floating nearby and tied it to the lifeboat's single mast. The sun came up and the desperate crew bailed and rowed, moving slowly in the direction toward what they hoped was land.

The men were tired and bruised from the crash. They squinted into the glaring Caribbean sun hoping for a sign of land. They were wet and hungry and not exactly sure where they were. Captain Hilton, who had been sick before any of this had even started, was getting worse by the minute.

There was nothing to eat and no fresh water to drink. After a full day of baking in the sun and not knowing where they were, the frightened men settled into their first night, the darkness covering everything—seven men packed into a small boat.

Hope flashed briefly when they felt the lifeboat's bottom hit something solid—could it be land? No! It was a large shark following the boat and the frightened crew, waiting for its next dinner.

At the sight of the shark, Captain Hilton lost what was left of his composure. He began sobbing and told the crew they would never survive, they would never reach land. They were lost forever, he told them.

A sobbing captain does not inspire confidence in a crew. The captain's hopelessness was contagious. He wasn't wrong. They were in a leaking boat that was barely floating, they had no food and no water, and they weren't even sure where they were. Things weren't looking good.

Daniel Collins would have none of that.

"We will hit land soon," he told the crew while Captain Hilton sobbed. "One more day at the most, and we'll reach land and we'll be fine." He didn't point out that Captain Hilton was going crazy, but he thought it, and he knew he had to take charge.

"Keep rowing," he told the crew. "We're close to land. Keep rowing and keep bailing."

And so they did, throughout the entire dark night. The seas began to flatten and the winds died down. As first light crawled over the eastern horizon, the exhausted crew spotted a small dot, just a fleck of what could be land in the distance.

By the time the light was stronger and the day warmer, they could hear it—the sound of waves crashing against a shore!

With the help of their feeble, makeshift sail, they floated very close to land, and after catching the top of a wave, they passed over a reef that protected Cruz del Padre, or Cross of the Father Island, a small island only a few miles wide.

The island was almost entirely surrounded by a mangrove swamp. Thick bushes rose as high as 15 feet, with tangled roots that dug deeply into the mud of the swamp. Those roots kept the island from washing away in powerful storms. The mangroves made the island look much larger than it really was.

But it was dry land. And that was all that mattered.

As they neared the brilliant white beach, the water became an inviting greenish-blue. Things were looking up! They were saved!

Or so it appeared.

Exhausted, but immensely relieved, the sailors pulled the boat up the beach as far as they could. They crawled out onto the warm sand.

It appeared they had landed on a place used by fishermen. There were huts and a small boat in the distance. Maybe fishermen used the place to store their catch while they waited until they had enough to take to Cuba, where it would fetch a nice price.

In the distance, beyond where the crew had passed over the reef, they spied the wrecks of two larger schooners. Maybe those ships were too large to have made it over the reef. The boats sat rotting in the sun, punished by the crashing waves and slowly breaking apart.

What had happened to the crews?

Soon, they spotted the fishermen themselves. Five of them were paddling a large log canoe to the beach. The crew of the *Betsey* had found not only a dry, safe island, but one with people who would help them get to Cuba.

The fishermen spotted the survivors. They paddled to the beach, stepped out, and walked over to the men from the *Betsey*, who sprawled on the sand, resting. The fishermen didn't speak English, but pointed to the two huts on a small hill near the center of the island. The grateful sailors and their new hosts walked to the huts.

The crew of the *Betsey* noticed the huts were built from planks taken from the wrecked ships. They were about 7 feet high and 15 feet long, with roofs made of thatched grass. Near one corner of the first hut, the fishermen had hung their nets out to dry in the hot island sun.

The fishermen brought the crew some much-need food—turtle meat and fish soup that had been stewing in a pot over a fire outside one of the huts.

The crew of the *Betsey* ate. Then, they spread out some sails that had been sitting nearby on the warm sand, and were soon fast asleep.

Except for Daniel Collins.

He felt uneasy about the situation. Something did not seem right. He did not trust the kindness of these fishermen. And he was not about to go to sleep. Perhaps it was the uneasiness from his bad dream, or maybe just his gut feeling, but he didn't like their hosts.

For one thing, these fishermen were all big and there was an edginess to their appearance. They all had scarred faces, long beards, and missing fingers and teeth. Was their appearance the result of fishing? Or was it maybe because of some rougher work?

When the crew fell asleep, the fishermen left. That's when Daniel Collins set out to explore the island.

He followed a small creek until it emptied into a large bay on the other side of the island, about a mile from the huts. In the bay, anchored just off the mouth of the creek in a small cove, he saw a larger sailing vessel—a schooner. Maybe that was the ship these fishermen used to take their catch to Cuba. Maybe these odd-looking fellows *are* fishermen, Daniel Collins thought.

But he doubted it.

He continued walking the shoreline, past the fishing schooner. He startled a large flock of beautiful flamingos, birds he had heard about but never seen. They flew off gracefully, but made such a racket that Daniel Collins became worried the fishermen would discover he was prying nosily around the island rather than sleeping in the hut.

He decided to head back. But not before noticing how lonely and isolated the island was. Anything could happen here and no one would ever know, he thought.

As he rounded a point on the beach near the anchored schooner, he decided to take a shortcut through the mangroves. He followed a path he had noticed earlier.

The thick trunks and exposed roots of the tall bushes were covered with shells of oysters that had latched on during storms. They cut him as quickly and neatly as razors, opening cuts on his arms and legs as easily as you would slice open a ripe melon. Soon, his feet, arms, and legs were coved with blood, his shirt and pants tattered. In the late morning heat, swarms of mosquitoes rose, attracted by the blood.

These mangrove swamps were no place to spend any time, he thought.

When Daniel Collins returned to the camp, he saw that the fishermen were back as well. This time, they weren't as polite or generous. They were acting as if the crew of the *Betsey* were interrupting some other work.

That night, he did not sleep again. Instead, he listened to the fishermen talking in low voices outside the hut. After what seemed like hours, the head fisherman came inside and extinguished a lamp that had been burning fish oil. It was completely dark.

The crew of the *Betsey* slept soundly. The man went back outside and picked up his conversation with his friends. Daniel Collins wondered, were they planning something for the next day? Something was going on.

The next morning, the fishermen's kindness seemed to have returned. They took the crew of the *Betsey* down a path to the creek Daniel Collins had found the day before and let the men know they could bathe. How kind of them, thought the crew.

Daniel Collins heard his crewmate Charles Manuel say something in Spanish to one of the fishermen. That's odd, he thought. Manuel had kept to himself the entire voyage. Daniel Collins did not know him very well. He wondered what they were saying, but did nothing.

Daniel Collins skipped the bath, even though his cuts and sores from the mangrove swamp could have used a cleaning. Instead, he walked around a spike of land just out of sight of his crewmates and the fishermen.

What he saw made every cell in his body long to run.

There, half buried in the sand, were skeletons. Human skeletons. They had been there a while. The bones were bleached white from the sun. Daniel Collins recognized ribs, fingers, legs, and hips—every part of the human body lay strewn about that beach, except for the skulls.

Where were the skulls?

Daniel Collins slipped back in with the crew of the *Betsey* before they noticed he was missing. When they returned to the hut, he pulled Captain Hilton aside and warned him to be very, very careful. "Do not trust these guys," Daniel Collins pleaded.

But the captain did not listen. He was tired from being sick the whole trip, tired from his breakdown in the lifeboat, tired from the rescue. "These fishermen will take us to Cuba," he told Daniel Collins.

Big mistake.

After a second peaceful night in the huts, the crew of the *Betsey* was awakened by the head fisherman early the next morning. "It is time to go to Cuba," he said in broken English. With that announcement, he rousted them all from their comfortable sleep.

As the crew of the *Betsey* and the fishermen stood outside the huts, Daniel Collins noticed the head fisherman pointing excitedly to something in the distance as he muttered to his friends. Daniel Collins followed the man's crooked finger and saw a strange-looking boat coming into view.

The head fisherman pulled his sharp machete from his belt, turned to the crew of the *Betsey,* then slowly brought the knife across his neck in a menacing gesture. Then he smiled.

As the boat closed in on the beach, Daniel Collins saw it was about 35 feet long, with an open deck. It was the strangest boat he had ever seen. Its hull was painted black, with a thin white stripe along the waterline. Inside, it was painted red. At various seats under a collection of small sails was a group of 10 men pulling strongly on long oars.

Their appearance was not comforting.

Each of the rowing, grunting men carried a musket. Each had a machete on a leather strap around his shoulders, and knives tucked into his belt. They looked as if they had not bathed in months.

Leading them off the boat was a man so enormous and so ugly that he could not possibly walk through a town without sending the citizens running. Below his left eye was a thick and bulging scar, where his face seemed to have been split open with the blade of a sharp and heavy sword. He was missing his front teeth and had no upper lip, which must have been taken off with the same sword stroke that gashed his face. His black beard reached to his bulging chest.

Daniel Collins had never seen anyone so large. He guessed this fearsome giant weighed almost 300 pounds. He was well armed, with pistols on each side, a musket in his arms, one knife in a scabbard on his side, and another strapped across his chest.

He was greeted warmly by the head fisherman.

They are friends, Daniel Collins thought. These people are pirates, not fishermen. We are their latest catch!

The ugly pirate acted quickly. He assigned three of his men to watch over the crew of the *Betsey,* who were standing on the beach with their mouths open. The head fisherman jumped aboard the pirates' boat, and in a very short time, the whole group was laughing and drinking from a bottle, passing it from man to snarling man.

Captain Hilton, always optimistic, seemed unable to understand what was about to happen. These rough men, now laughing as they stood over the crew of the *Betsey,* were not friends. They were not about to take them to Cuba.

In fact, they were about to kill them.

The men in the boat continued to pass the bottle around, each taking long gulps. Daniel Collins looked around frantically, trying to find a way to escape.

Captain Hilton, still smiling and hoping, finally seemed to grasp that these men in the boat, drinking whatever it was they were drinking, were not friends.

The men surrounded Captain Hilton. Maybe he could tell them where he'd hidden his money.

Captain Hilton's smile disappeared. He had nothing! It had all been lost when the *Betsey* struck the reef and sank.

The pirates began pummeling Captain Hilton with the butts of their muskets, twisting his head, and punching him with their fists. The crew of the *Betsey* could only watch in shocked silence, the truth of their situation plain to all of them. They finally realized that their new friends were not friends at all.

Daniel Collins was flabbergasted at the cruelty of these men. They showed no mercy to Captain Hilton, who was pleading for his life. With no thought to the consequences, Daniel Collins stood and screamed at them to stop.

For that he was struck quickly with the back end of a musket and sent to the ground, dazed and stunned.

While the captain's beating continued, the grimy pirates kept looking toward the shocked crew and drawing their knives across their own throats, smiling with menace.

After a good minute of beating, the head pirate had his men surround the crew. The pirates marched them under close guard down the path Daniel Collins had taken on his earlier exploration of the island.

Daniel Collins quickly recognized that they were heading toward the beach where he had seen the headless skeletons. This was not comforting.

As they marched along the narrow trail, the pirates began pulling long knives and machetes from their belts. They grinned and gawked like they were preparing for Christmas dinner.

The crew of the *Betsey* began to pray. It was a sad and mournful sound, these men pleading to God to save them, pleading to the pirates for mercy. Yet they marched along in an orderly fashion, like sheep to the slaughter.

The pirates laughed at the men. Then they began to sing.

One looked at Captain Hilton and said in broken English, "You will soon be sliced like a good piece of beef!"

Daniel Collins knew he needed to jump suddenly and break free to escape. But he saw no opening. The sad crew and the boisterous pirates marched for about a mile.

It was the last mile the crew of the *Betsey* would ever walk.

When they rounded a point that jutted out to sea, the pirates told the group to stop. Daniel Collins saw, to his horror, that they were at the very place he had seen the skeletons. He knew what was about to happen. In that moment, he felt what he would later describe to the people back in Maine as "the stillness of death."

And then it began.

The crew of the *Betsey* exchanged horrified glances, their last goodbyes to each other. They all knew what was about to happen and they could do nothing to prevent it.

The frail Captain Hilton was first.

A burly pirate forced the captain to his knees on the warm sand, roughly grabbed the hair on the back of his head, and pulled back sharply, exposing the captain's thin neck. Everyone turned away, but they all heard the captain shriek with horror as the pirate drew his sword and brought it down on the captain's exposed throat. One hard thrust was enough to leave the captain's head attached only by a thin tendon. His screams became a gurgle as his dying breath left his lungs. The pirate made one more quick slice and suddenly he held the captain's head above the crumpled body on the bloody sand.

He walked to the water's edge and tossed it in the bay.

Blood was everywhere.

The captain's screams had sent a flock of flamingos nesting in the nearby trees upward into a vast, moving cloud of white and pink.

The first mate, Joshua Merry, was next. He looked at his pirate executioner one last time in a plea for mercy. It did no good. The pirate lopped off Joshua Merry's head as his companions cheered. To add a bit of flourish, he ran his sword into Joshua Merry's stomach, spilling his guts onto the beach.

After Joshua Merry, the slaughter of Seth Russel, Benjamin Bridge, and Detrey Jerome followed—one after another in quick, bloody succession. Only Charles Manuel and Daniel Collins remained.

Daniel Collins, sitting so close to the massacre, was covered in blood. He knew he was next and he knew he had no time to plead for mercy.

The pirate standing behind him grabbed Daniel Collins by his hair and snapped back his head, trying to expose his throat for the final and fatal slice of the knife.

Then, something happened that Daniel Collins would always say was his greatest moment of luck. The pirate swung his sword and missed, hitting Daniel Collins's jaw instead of the soft meat of his neck. The blow stunned Daniel Collins, but for only a second. He knew he had to act.

He jumped to his feet and ran into the nearby mangrove swamp. The entire pirate crew was so astonished by this that they stood motionless, staring. No one had ever missed before. It was all the time Daniel Collins needed. Once he stepped into the darkness of the swamp, his chances of survival increased dramatically.

Inside the gloom of the swamp, Daniel Collins began running for his life as fast as he could through mud, water, and tangled roots. Taking a quick look back at the scene on the beach, he saw Charles Manuel running off in another direction. He noticed that none of the pirates bothered to chase Mr. Manuel. How odd, he thought.

With the shrieks and dying screams of his companions still ringing in his ears, Daniel Collins went deeper into the swamp.

If Cross of the Father Island had been a barren, treeless place, he would not have survived two minutes. The pirates would have chased him down and taken his head, chucking it into the water with the others.

And they would have done so angrily, he was sure of that.

But Daniel Collins was saved by the thickness of the swamp, which offered many places to duck and hide.

Standing up to his waist in the thick, muddy water, Daniel Collins's legs and arms and feet were again sliced open by the sharp shells on the trees and roots. The mosquitoes began to take their first painful bites. Bleeding and horrified by what he had just seen, Daniel Collins counted his blessings.

But it wasn't over yet. The chase was on.

He was in a very tough spot. He watched the pirates rush into the swamp, missing him by no more than 20 feet as he ducked into the water. They couldn't see him with only his face exposed above the surface.

For the rest of the day, Daniel Collins crept through the swamp, crouching so the water was up to his neck. He was barefoot and sore and bleeding. He stayed quiet as he heard the pirates yelling to each other, asking if they had seen anything.

It was a long and tense day, but the longer Daniel Collins stayed in the swamp, the more chance he had of staying hidden.

At sunset, Daniel Collins found himself alone and still alive. He had worked his way through the swamp across the entire island. He could see a white beach. Across a stretch of water to the east, he could see another island. He could no longer hear the shouting of the pirates.

He spent the night on the edge of the beach, hidden in the thickness of some reeds. He was safe, at least for the night.

As the sun rose the next morning, Daniel Collins quietly slipped off his torn and blood-stained pants and shirt, tied them in a bundle to carry, and slipped silently into the water.

He said a prayer and began swimming to the island across the bay.

Daniel Collins had always been a good swimmer. He had made use of the brief Maine summers and spent as much time as he could in the water.

The habit served him well off Cross of the Father Island. He made it to the first beach and crawled ashore. He was exhausted. His bleeding arms and legs stung badly from the saltwater.

Mosquitoes favored any open skin, which was pretty much all of it, given how ragged his shirt and pants were.

As he sat on that first beach, he caught his breath. He saw another island in the distance. He knew that with each new island he reached, the safer he'd be from the pirates.

He swam to the next island. And the next.

That night, Daniel Collins made a discovery that helped him stay alive. Starving, he had lifted a mossy rock that sat above the tide line and flicked off a piece of kelp that had attached itself. Underneath the rock was a crawfish, a small whiskery sea creature not unlike a shrimp, or maybe a cockroach. He quickly tossed it into his mouth and felt its tendrils still wriggling as it went down. It was the nutrition he needed to survive.

The next day, he swam some more. He thought about what the pirates would do if they found him and that gave him enough energy to keep swimming.

On his second night after escaping, curled up on a strange, lonely beach far from home and the Maine he loved, Daniel Collins had a dream. It was the first of the nightmares he would suffer for the rest of his life. He would never be able to escape it, try as he might.

In the dream, he saw his headless crewmates on the bloody beach of Cross of the Father Island. He saw the slaughter and heard the screams again and again.

The next morning, thinking of Maine, he stepped into the water and swam again. For four exhausting, painful days, Daniel Collins swam from island to island. Altogether, he swam close to 11 miles.

His final swim took him to a wide beach that stretched for miles. Was it Cuba? He was so weak, he had no idea. He only knew he was safe from the pirates. Daniel Collins had no energy left. He could swim no more.

He crawled up that last beach and followed a small path alongside a clean, clear creek running into the sea. He was so tired that he had to use tree limbs for support as he pulled himself along the path.

Daniel Collins lost track of time and sat down, unsure if he could go any farther, wondering if his last breath would take place under a tree on an island far from Wiscasset. He was so tired that he almost did not care.

So be it, he thought.

He drifted into a troubled sleep, the dream about his bloody and headless crewmates descending on him once again. For the rest of his life, Daniel Collins would never be able to erase the screams and the horrors from his mind. The sounds and the blood of that lonely beach were burned forever into his memory.

He was awakened by a noise he had not heard in weeks—the sound of a horse's snort. On the horse was a man, looking curiously at this bloody and scarred mystery man, sleeping under a tree.

The man approached cautiously, then reached into his saddle bag and offered Daniel Collins a drink of water from his pouch.

Daniel Collins looked up, puzzled.

Then it sunk in. He was saved.

The man who found Daniel Collins worked for the owner of a large plantation on Cuba. He had been on a ride to check the wealthy man's estate. He took Daniel Collins to his owner's large mansion, where Daniel Collins was fed and cleaned, and where he stayed until he was healthy enough to go to Matanzas, a city in Cuba. In Matanzas, he saw Charles Manuel, the only other crew member of the *Betsey* to survive. Daniel Collins never gave up his suspicion that the pirates had let Charles Manuel go free for some reason he never learned. After some more time recovering in Matanzas, Daniel Collins boarded a ship, the *Shamrock*, for passage back to Maine. In April 1825, he arrived back in Wiscasset.

It is unknown if he ever went to sea again.

WHAT ELSE IS GOING ON IN THE 1820s?

- In March 1825, John Quincy Adams is sworn in as the sixth president of the United States of America.

- Ezra Daggett and his nephew, Thomas Kensett, discover a way to store food in cans. This would have greatly improved the diets of the men on the *Betsey* while at sea.

- A man named Walter Hunt invents the safety pin.

- The Erie Canal, which links New York City to the Great Lakes and the land beyond, is finally finished. It opens up commerce to a wide, unexplored part of the growing United States of America.

- Maine has been a part of the United States of America for only four years when the *Betsey* sets sail.

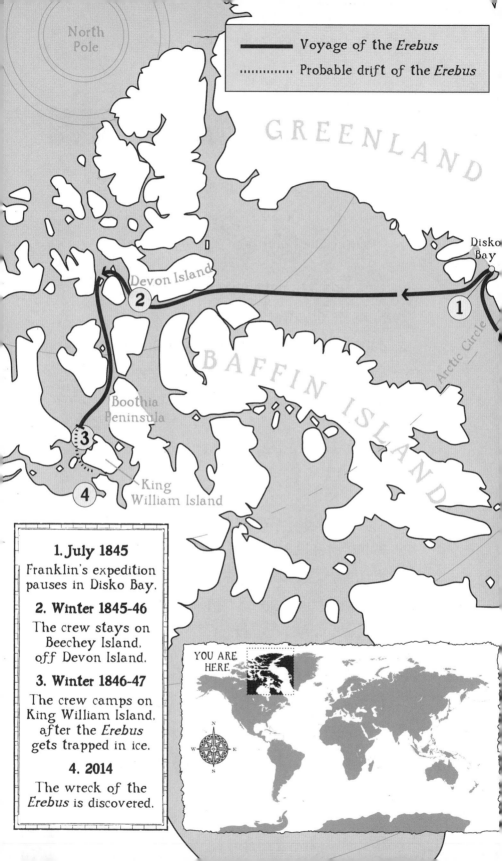

North Pole

GREENLAND

Disko Bay

Voyage of the *Erebus*
············ Probable drift of the *Erebus*

Devon Island

②

①

Arctic Circle

BAFFIN ISLAND

Boothia Peninsula

③

④

King William Island

1. July 1845
Franklin's expedition pauses in Disko Bay.

2. Winter 1845-46
The crew stays on Beechey Island, off Devon Island.

3. Winter 1846-47
The crew camps on King William Island, after the *Erebus* gets trapped in ice.

4. 2014
The wreck of the *Erebus* is discovered.

YOU ARE HERE

N W E S

Chapter Two

Searching for Captain Franklin

The Canadian Arctic is frozen solid most of the year. During the short periods when narrow passages thaw, they become a twisted, frozen, terror-filled maze that changes on the whims of weather and tide. A calm three miles of sea one day could be frozen solid the next. A clear passage on Monday might be so thickly covered in fog on Wednesday that you can't see the tip of your nose. There are also menacing polar bears that can take off your head with the flick of one paw. Large ice floes can crush a boat as easily as you might crumple a tissue. That is what Captain Sir John Franklin faced during his 1845 expedition, and that is what likely killed him and his crew. But was it so horrible that it forced them into terrible acts in the end?

It is no small matter when a hero disappears without a trace, leaving nothing but rumors about his fate.

Captain Sir John Franklin and his crew of 128 men left England in 1845 to find the fabled and elusive Northwest Passage through Arctic Canada. Many felt the Northwest Passage would be the fastest route to Asia and all its riches.

Hundreds had already died trying to sail their way through crushing ice and dead ends that froze them in place until they starved to death.

Captain Franklin's departure was filled with acclaim and great hope. He and his crew were brave to even attempt such a difficult journey. And then—they disappeared. What became of Captain Franklin and the crews of his two ships?

How did such a large and heroic group of Englishmen simply vanish from the face of the earth?

For years, there was no word from Captain Franklin or any of his crew. The world doubted that they were still alive. The Canadian Arctic, with its cruel climate, was an unsympathetic killer. Were Captain Franklin and his men swallowed by some unknown Arctic phenomenon? Had they met slow and painful deaths, out of food and out of hope? Had they gone out in a blaze of glory? Perhaps they had even accomplished the impossible mission!

Many explorers tried to find answers, and some of the answers they found were horrifying. One early explorer found graves on Beechey Island, located in the frigid maze of islands and channels that Captain Franklin would have had to pass through. After that, nothing else was learned from explorers until 1854, nine years after Captain Franklin and his ships had left England.

That year, Arctic explorer John Rae returned to Britain with news that shook the country to its core. What he reported blared from the front pages of every newspaper in England.

It was as if John Rae had poked a sharp stick into a hornet's nest.

Captain Franklin and his crew were all dead, John Rae revealed to eager ears. That news was feared, but expected. But John Rae added a macabre twist to the tale.

Some of the crew survived longer than others.

On his trip, John Rae spoke with the Inuit, natives of the far north, who had described the gruesome scene they had come across during a hunting trip. They told John Rae that they had spotted mutilated bodies and kettles holding what looked like human stew. Captain Franklin and his men had become cannibals, driven by their torturous journey to eat horrific meals. They had consumed the flesh of their dead companions to stay alive.

"It is evident," John Rae told reporters, "that our wretched countrymen had been driven to the last dread alternative—cannibalism—as a means of prolonging existence."

This was outrageous news to the English, who worshipped Captain John Franklin. It was worse news to Lady Jane Franklin, who, of course, preferred to be known as the widow of a hero, not the widow of a man who had eaten his crew. She found the rumor that her husband and his men were cannibals hard to swallow.

She responded to the clamor by insisting that her husband and his brave crew were actually murdered by the natives who had made those impossible claims. She even got the famous writer Charles Dickens to say in newspapers published all over England that the Inuit were "a gross handful of uncivilized people, with a domesticity of blood and blubber."

And John Rae was no better, Lady Franklin hinted. She let it be known that John Rae was an annoyance, a pest, a liar who had relied on the stories of strangers to smear the reputation of John Franklin.

In 1857, she chose Francis Leopold McClintock to travel to the frozen Arctic and put an end to the malicious talk. He would go to the Arctic and disprove the despicable rumors—and Captain Franklin would once again be a hero for the ages.

Lady Franklin found no problem in raising money for another expedition. She purchased a 177-ton, steam-powered ship called the *Fox*, which was small but maneuverable.

Captain McClintock had been to the Arctic before, and had managed to return. That alone spoke well of his instincts and knowledge.

Captain McClintock was afraid of nothing, and he had a way of making the men who joined him just as courageous. They needed to be. Men would die on this trip—they always did—and everyone knew it. He and his crew had to be willing to suffer the same fate as Captain Franklin, whatever that had been.

A calm and reasonable leader, Captain McClintock had left his native Ireland and joined the British navy at age 13. He once saved a ship and its officers from being swallowed up in a storm, which earned him a promotion. A historian described him as having "a short, slender, but wiry and muscular frame well fitted for the endurance of long-continued exertion and hardships."

With a crew of 25 men aboard the *Fox*, Captain McClintock set sail from Aberdeen, Scotland, in July 1857. It had been 12 years since anyone had seen Captain Franklin and his men.

When they got to the Arctic, they were met with what polar experts described as bad ice—a winter so cold that travel was impossible. That first winter, they were frozen in for eight months.

Eight months of being stuck in a solid landscape of ice and snow! They were so cold that their joints and limbs ached all the time. Their eyes hurt from straining in the constant dark. Their skin grew cracked and sore from the dry conditions. Death was a daily possibility.

As the winter of 1858 finally began to fade, Captain McClintock and his men began a series of excursions to find out what had happened to Captain Franklin. Captain McClintock was an expert in Arctic travel, skilled at moving across the ice on sleds led by dogs. He knew how to keep his men and the dogs fit. He taught them how to read the signs that others ignored at their peril. Captain McClintock was a master of training and motivation and worked his men hard.

What they found would be etched in history. Whether it was correct or not is still being debated more than 150 years later.

In August 1858, the seekers reached Beechey Island and built a large cairn, a carefully created pile of rocks and stones. Into the cairn, they installed a marble plaque commissioned by Lady Franklin as a memorial to her husband and his crew. It read in part:

TO THE MEMORY OF
FRANKLIN,
CROZIER, FITZJAMES,
AND ALL THEIR
GALLANT BROTHER OFFICERS AND
FAITHFUL
COMPANIONS WHO HAVE SUFFERED AND
PERISHED
IN THE CAUSE OF SCIENCE AND
THE SERVICE OF THEIR COUNTRY.
THIS TABLET
IS ERECTED NEAR THE SPOT WHERE
THEY PASSED THEIR FIRST ARCTIC
WINTER, AND WHENCE THEY ISSUED
FORTH TO CONQUER DIFFICULTIES OR
TO DIE.

There was nothing on this marble memorial that mentioned cannibalism, of course.

The crew left Beechey Island and sailed into Lancaster Sound, where travel was often measured in yards rather than miles. Captain McClintock described it with no great affection.

"All Sunday the gale continued, although not with such extreme force; the deep rolling of the ship, and moaning of the half-drowned dogs amidst the pelting sleet and rain, was anything but agreeable. Notwithstanding that I had been up all the previous night, I felt too anxious to sleep; the wind blew directly up Barrow Strait, drifting us about two miles an hour. Occasionally she drifted to leeward of masses of ice, reminding us that if any of the dense pack which covered this sea only three weeks ago remained to leeward of us, we must be rapidly setting down upon its weather edge. The only expedient in such a case is to endeavor to run into it—once well within its outer margin a ship is comparatively safe—the danger lies in the attempt to penetrate; to escape out of the pack afterwards is also a doubtful matter."

They moved further and further into the territory where Captain Franklin had last been seen, then stalled again in the winter of 1858–1859.

Being frozen in ice in complete Arctic darkness for months on end is not for the faint of heart. Men imagine all sorts of horrors in the dark— crews of the past back from the dead, voices in the whipping wind, the cries of wives and babies left back home.

It was enough to drive even the bravest man utterly crazy.

Captain McClintock was not a commander who allowed his crew to sit still. They practiced building snow shelters in temperatures that dropped to 40 degrees below zero—low enough to kill a man who ventured outside unprotected. They hunted on the ice for meat and pelts. They shot a massive polar bear and took its pelt aboard as a present for their sponsor, Lady Franklin.

More than anything, the crew stayed patient. Impatience and rash moves were the killers to be wary of in this environment.

Two men died, one from injuries after a fall, the other of what they called apoplexy, which is similar to a stroke. While sad, this was a pretty low number for an Arctic expedition.

Arctic nights were not just depressing. The average temperature was 20 degrees below zero. It was not suitable for strolls outside to stretch the legs and get way from annoying crewmates on the cramped ship.

And through it all, ghosts were slowly beginning to emerge.

In March 1859, on a brief sled trip outside the *Fox* as the Arctic night slowly grew warmer and just a hint of light began to show, a member of the crew met an Inuit seal hunter. He was wearing a gold button that could only have come from a British naval uniform. Later, they purchased silverware and more buttons from other Inuit. Captain Franklin's crew was beginning to reveal itself.

It was not until the spring thaw of 1859—thaw being a very relative word in the Arctic—that Captain McClintock and his second in command, William Hobson, set out. They began a trip that would start to fit the jagged pieces of the puzzle together. Some of the truth of what had happened began to appear.

That spring, Captain McClintock and William Hobson searched for what they called "the fatal march of the lost crews." They looked on the west coast of King William Island.

They traveled at night to prevent sun blindness as the harsh and unrelenting Arctic sun began to rise. They collected stories and artifacts that were clearly from Captain Franklin's ships. It was almost as if the ghosts of Captain Franklin's men had left a trail of breadcrumbs. Among the items they found to bring back to England were six pieces of silver plate bearing the family crests or initials of Captain Franklin and his officers.

On May 24, the ghostly trail yielded a human skeleton. Next to it lay a small notebook.

Captain McClintock wrote, "This victim was a young man, slightly built, and perhaps above the common height; the dress appeared to be that of a steward or officer's servant, the loose bow-knot in which his neck-handkerchief was tied not being used by seamen or officers."

Walking along the top of a ridge, the man had dropped to the ground face first and died.

One of their discoveries a week later told more of the grim tale. On May 30, William Hobson found a large boat on a desolate beach, what Captain McClintock called "another melancholy relic." It was surrounded by "a vast quantity of tattered clothing."

Captain McClintock thought that the boat weighed close to 800 pounds. Maybe Captain Franklin's crew had loaded it up in an attempt to find a way out of their deadly predicament. Could they have been pushing the boat over the ice, hoping to find open water?

What they found inside the boat was more shocking. Skeletons!

"There was that in the boat which transfixed us with awe. It was portions of two human skeletons. One was that of a slight young person; the other of a large, strongly-made, middle-aged man."

One skeleton had been ravaged by a wild animal, but the other was in very good shape and covered in clothes and furs. Those clothes and furs couldn't do a thing to help that skeleton stay warm, now.

Scattered around the boat were five watches and two double-barrel shotguns. There were also five or six books, including a small Bible. There were eight pairs of boots, silk handkerchiefs, towels, soap, a sponge, a toothbrush, hair combs, a mackintosh gun-cover, twine, nails, saws, files, bristles, powder, bullets, shot, cartridges, a leather cartridge-case, and knives.

It was a strange collection of things.

The collection reminded the men of a regular and safe life. What a bizarre sight on a cold, lonely island thousands of miles from home.

Perhaps the boat meant Captain Franklin's men had not lost all hope. Maybe they were ready to push the boat into the sea at the proper time to hunt for food and possibly a route out of the misery in which they were trapped. Except—what was missing? Food. There was very little food.

By the time the dead men attempted to get the boat to water, they must have been starving.

"The only provisions we could find were tea and chocolate; of the former very little remained, but there were nearly 40 pounds of the latter. These articles alone could never support life in such a climate, and we found neither biscuit nor meat of any kind. A portion of tobacco and an empty pemmican-tin, capable of containing 22 pounds weight, were discovered. The tin was marked with an E; it had probably belonged to the 'Erebus.' None of the fuel originally brought from the ships remained in or about the boat, but there was no lack of it, for a drift-tree was lying on the beach close at hand, and had the party been in need of fuel they would have used the paddles and bottom-boards of the boat."

The boat on that empty beach was an eloquent portrait of men nearing the ends of their lives, but still trying. Perhaps, though, they knew there could not be much hope left.

On May 5, William Hobson and his crew made the most chilling discovery: They found a stone cairn erected by Captain Franklin's men. Among the stones, they discovered weathered messages written nearly a year apart by crew members. Initially, there was no indication of despair or hopelessness. There was no call for pity.

The first message, written on May 28, 1847, was hopeful, full of vitality and energy. It said that *Erebus* and *Terror* had spent the winter locked in ice off King William Island. "Sir John Franklin commanding the Expedition. All well," the message said.

The second message was a death knell, dated nearly a year later, on April 25, 1848. Just a short few sentences filled with despair and resignation that death was not far off. It was written on the same sheet of paper as the first, in the margins. It told another, darker story. It said that *Erebus* and *Terror* had been trapped in the ice for a year and a half and that the crew had abandoned the ships on April 22. Captain Franklin was dead, and so were more than 20 others. The rest of the crew, now down to 105 men, set out the next day in search of salvation.

It was a salvation that never came.

The final journey of Captain Franklin's crew did not end well, it seemed. Captain McClintock recorded his shock: "In the short space of twelve months how mournful had become the history of Franklin's expedition."

Around the cairn where William Hobson had pulled the chilling note were "quantities of clothing and articles of all kinds lying about the cairn, as if these men, aware that they were retreating for their lives, had there abandoned everything which they considered superfluous."

The desperate survivors were courageous to the last. They didn't lie down and wait for death, but headed into the vast whiteness as if they were defying nature itself.

In all of his reports, Captain McClintock never made any mention of the possibility of cannibalism. But if the lost members of the expedition had turned in desperation to eating the flesh of their dead companions, who is to judge?

In the end it did not matter. They all died.

Captain McClintock's discoveries proved that Captain Franklin and his men were heroes. Doomed heroes, yes, but brave men all the same.

Captain McClintock returned home in September 1859 to great praise. His story of the valiant crews of Captain Sir John Franklin allowed the English public to breathe a deep sigh of relief. They could forget John Rae and his horrible claims of cannibalism. They surely didn't want to dig too deeply into whether they were true.

Captain McClintock summed it up and tied it neatly with a bow. In 1860, he was knighted by the queen for his efforts.

The full picture of what happened to Captain Franklin and his crew, where and when, is still evolving. In 1981, a team led by anthropologist Owen Beattie exhumed the graves on Beechey Island. He found other artifacts over the years. His findings: The men had died of starvation and pneumonia, not surprising, given the horrible conditions they were exposed to. Beattie also found something that had not been thought of before. The men's deaths were likely sped up by the poorly preserved food in tins they brought along or by the water system on board the ship.

The most stunning breakthrough came in 2014, when an expedition found one of Captain Franklin's sunken ships still preserved in the icy waters of the Canadian Arctic, near Queen Maud Gulf. It was identified as the *Erebus*. Research continues today. People still wonder: Did they resort to cannibalism?

WHAT ELSE IS GOING ON IN 1845?

- *The Raven*, a narrative poem by American writer Edgar Allen Poe, is published.

- Florida is admitted as the 27th state in the United States of America, and Texas becomes the 28th state.

- Stephen Perry finalizes his patent for rubber bands. What was used to hold things together before then?

- James K. Polk is sworn in as the 11th president of the United States of America.

ATLANTIC OCEAN

FLORIDA

GULF of MEXICO

BAHAMAS

CUBA

HISPANIOLA

JAMAICA

PUERTO RICO

CARIBBEAN SEA

Early 1700s
Anne Bonny and Mary Read sailed the seas around Cuba, Jamaica, and the Bahamas with Calico Jack Rackham.

YOU ARE HERE

N
W   E
S

Chapter Three

Fiercer Than Most Men

How did an innocent girl from a small English town become one of the most feared pirates in the Caribbean? How did she come to replace childhood days of helping her mother with an adult life helping the truly awful Calico Jack Rackham raid and plunder unsuspecting ships near Jamaica?

Mary Read's story is a very curious one indeed, with more twists and turns than there were dark alleys in the town of Plymouth, England, which she first called home.

Mary Read did not wake one morning and decide to become a sword-swinging, gun-toting member of Calico Jack Rackham's motley crew. This sort of transformation takes a while. Growing from a rough-and-tumble kid into a pirate with a nasty reputation requires a series of fateful choices made during a lifetime.

Mary Read's journey of pretending began almost from the moment she was born in Plymouth, England, around 1690. Plymouth was a small town outside of London, which was a large, bustling city, even back then.

Most of Mary Read's relatives lived in London. The relatives had money, and they longed to see her older brother, Mark, who was not even a year old at the time. Mary Read's mother wanted nothing to do with them, though. She was the widow of a sea captain and she was pregnant with another man's baby.

Soon after Mary Read was born, her brother died. Back then, nearly a third of children died before reaching their 15th birthday. Diseases, accidents, and starvation made survival a tricky business for kids.

Mary Read's mother was a quick thinker. She came up with a plan that would allow her and her newborn daughter to get the help they needed.

Shortly after Mark Read died, she wrote to the relatives in London. "I'm sorry that I have been avoiding you in Plymouth," she wrote. "I want to come to London with my son, who needs your help. I realize I cannot help him on my own."

Then she dressed Mary Read in boys' clothes and brought her to London to meet the family.

A grandmother, the sea captain's mother, gave them an allowance and a small bit of security because she thought the child was Mark Read. The only catch? Mary Read would have to keep dressing like a boy to keep up the charade!

Mary Read must have been good at pretending to be a boy. She must have been good with her fists and her wits to survive those knockabout days in London. The fact is, boys had easier lives than girls in those times. Boys were more valuable and they were less likely to be bothered by the rough characters who roamed the streets of the city.

Mary Read proved herself equal to other boys and, not surprisingly, smarter. She was living a lie in difficult circumstances, but her mind was quick. Mary Read instinctively knew how to adapt to anything.

This is terrific training for a future pirate.

The generous grandmother died before Mary Read reached her teens. Without the grandmother's money coming in, life became harder. Once again, Mary Read's mother thought quickly. She found the child a job as a servant, called a footman, with a French woman living in London.

This might seem something of a cushy job, helping a wealthy woman go about her daily chores, perhaps enjoying the life of the upper class. It wasn't. A domestic servant did not have an easy life, no matter if they were working for a duke or an earl or a wealthy French woman.

History records show that Mary Read did the job and did it well. Her training as a resourceful boy on the streets of London must have given her plenty of practice at moving furniture, running errands, doing laundry, cleaning, emptying chamber pots, and generally being available for anything.

Servants worked very long hours, seven days a week. They were paid poorly, sometimes with only a place to sleep and meals to eat. Did Mary Read like her job? Was she happy?

Nobody knows, and nobody ever will.

Maybe she became irritated by the daily grind of helping the rich woman, with no future of excitement in sight. Mary Read craved excitement. By the time she was in her teens, she was too feisty to continue to take orders from a boring old woman.

After she left the Frenchwoman, Mary Read enlisted in the British navy, still pretending to be a boy. She signed up as a powder monkey on a man o' war, a large ship with as many as 120 cannons of all sizes. Her job was carrying bags of gunpowder up from the hold of the ship to the cannon crew. She was only 13 and must have been pretty strong to heave that weight.

Since England was at war, Mary Read got her full measure of adventure. A British sailor once described life on a man o' war as "exhaustion and boredom punctuated by moments of terror."

During battles, sailors had to spread sand on deck to prevent the hustling crews from slipping on large pools of slick blood. When fired, the large cannons shook so violently that they had to be tied down with thick ropes. Sailors knew not to walk near them as they went off, or they would be knocked 20 yards away and break an arm or a leg or worse.

The air was thick with acrid smoke and the screams of wounded sailors. The men at the cannons screamed insults at the enemy, who might be drifting only 50 yards away.

The excitement of battle made Mary Read's heart race and she did her job well. In battle, she was in constant motion.

It was certainly a step up from cleaning the Frenchwoman's chamber pot!

There was a problem with life on board the ship, though. When not in battle, it was just as boring as being the Frenchwoman's servant.

Mary Read had to eat biscuits so old and moldy that she had to knock them on the deck to chase out the bugs. The water she drank was stored in moldy barrels and quickly turned green and foul tasting. If anyone complained, they would be flogged. Sailors were tied to the mast and whipped for even the smallest sign of disobedience.

So Mary Read jumped ship to find new ways to satisfy her thirst for adventure.

After she snuck away from the man o' war, Mary Read joined the British army and went to the region of Flanders, a Dutch-speaking English ally that was also fighting the French. By now, she was older and pretending to be a man instead of a boy.

Mary Read proved to be good in battle—she was deft with her sword and skilled at slicing off the enemy's arms and running through the attackers as they charged. She was very good on horseback, too, a skilled rider who won praise from her fellow soldiers and even some respect from the French.

Her deadly skills with the sword would prove very useful later in her life.

Mary Read never expected to find love on the battlefield, but that's exactly what happened. She fell in love with a soldier from Flanders, even though there wasn't a lot of time or space for affection in the barracks and tents where the soldiers lived. The object of her crush was astounded when she revealed to him that, first, she was a woman, and, second, that she was in love with him.

He got over his surprise pretty quickly, and fell in love with her as well. This made it difficult to live together and do soldierly things. They resigned from the army, said goodbye to war and fighting, and Mary Read put on a dress. The two got married and opened an inn called The Three Horses, located near the Castle Breda in Holland.

If this were a fairy tale, our story would end here, with Mary Read and her new husband living happily ever after. But this is not a fairy tale.

Very shortly after opening the inn, Mary Read's husband became ill and died. She was alone once again. Saddened, but undaunted, Mary Read did what she had always done—she pulled on some pants. Her brief period of living as a woman ended abruptly, because Mary Read knew that life was much easier for men.

Her next decision was a life-changing one: She hopped aboard a Dutch ship bound for the West Indies. It was in the warm Caribbean islands that she would find her fame and her true calling.

On the way to the islands, her ship was captured by English pirates led by a man named Calico Jack Rackham. Thinking she was a fellow Englishman, the pirates encouraged her to join them in capturing other ships and stealing as much as they could.

Mary Read thought it sounded like a great idea.

On board the pirate ship, she stared across the deck and discovered a pair of sparkling eyes set in the face of Anne Bonny, another woman dressed as a man. Mary Read's life would never be the same again.

Mary Read was like the gunpowder she had lugged aboard the man o' war not so long ago. Gunpowder is dangerous only when touched by fire. Anne Bonny was the fire to Mary Read's gunpowder. Together, they exploded across the Caribbean, leaving as much damage as a real cannon.

Mary Read and Anne Bonny shared many things. Both were women in a man's world. Both thirsted for adventure and hated boredom. Both were afraid of nothing. After they got to know each other better, they learned that they both liked making good impressions on men—into the tops of their heads with sharp swords.

Calico Jack was shocked to discover that his new crewman was actually a woman, but Mary Read proved herself worthy. She fought as hard as any of the men and quickly showed her ruthless side.

Mary Read and Anne Bonny formed a terrific killing team.

They were unlike anything people had seen in those days, when women were still considered the weaker gender. Alone, each proved she was capable of terrible things, but together, they fed off each other and became even more violent.

Anyone who had the misfortune of dealing with them realized pretty quickly it would have been better to avoid their lethal paths.

Like Mary Read, Anne Bonny was creative and clever. She had launched her own pirate career by mangling the limbs of a dressmaker's mannequin and smearing it with fake blood to make it look like a corpse. When the crew of a passing French merchant ship spotted Anne Bonny wielding an ax over her creation, they surrendered their cargo without a fight.

Anne Bonny and Mary Read were a match made in pirate heaven.

During their attacks on other ships, the pair wore loose tunics and wide trousers, pistols tucked in sashes around their waists, large, flashing sabers, and caps to hide their long hair. Witnesses were shocked when they learned the cursing, whirling pirates were actually women.

Calico Jack loved their raucous charms and ignored one of the first rules of being a pirate—no girls allowed. It was considered bad luck to have a woman on a pirate ship, never mind two.

The infamous pirate Blackbeard banned women from his ship. If his crew took one captive, she was strangled and pitched over the side.

Anne Bonny and Mary Read refused to be discouraged, and captured whatever there was of Calico Jack's pirate heart. They both fought with a frenzy that drew praise from their fellow pirates. And if anyone complained?

Anne Bonny might just silence them with a stab through the heart.

In one month, Anne Bonny and Mary Read took over seven fishing boats and two sloops near Jamaica, where they often hid in coves covered by thick mangroves. This kept them out of the sight of the nosy government ships that had begun to patrol the waters looking for them. A few weeks later, the women led a raid against a schooner, shooting at the crew as they climbed aboard.

That was when they made their first mistake: They held their captives for two days and then released them. The released prisoners returned to Jamaica with stories of the two fierce women.

Those stories attracted the wrong kind of attention. The governor's ships looked even harder for them.

Pirates were bad for the governor's business.

Every pirate knew that if they were caught, their lives would end quickly while they dangled in a tight noose at the end of a rope. Some might have been scared by that knowledge, but such thoughts rarely stopped pirates from fighting or pillaging and making their victims' lives miserable. That is what pirates did. Mary Read and Anne Bonny didn't find the threat of dangling from the end of a rope frightening at all.

Nothing seemed to slow them down when they were at their peak. Mary Read and Anne Bonny were mean women who loved nothing more than a good raid and all the riches it brought.

But Mary Read had a bad habit of picking the wrong time and place to fall in love. This time, a young sailor from one of the ships they'd attacked caught her eye. In the midst of all the raiding and violence and danger, Mary Read and the man fell in love.

The budding romance did not go over well with a fellow pirate who thought Mary Read was exactly what he wanted in a girlfriend. But Mary Read did not have a great deal of patience with her jealous crewmate. She broke his heart—by killing him. And unlike the last time she fell in love, she decided not to settle down and live a normal, boring life. She liked being a pirate, and she liked her partner, Anne Bonny. She didn't want to give it up.

Unfortunately, it wasn't up to her.

While Mary Read and Anne Bonny were collecting a large fortune from their raids, they were leaving behind a trail of evidence and rumors. Their bad reputation made it easy for the governor to follow them.

The authorities collected stories from disgruntled survivors of pirate attacks, who described Calico Jack and his "she devils." They began to learn Calico Jack's habits—where he preferred to rob, when he liked to attack, and in what direction he sailed afterward.

If you are a pirate, this is not a good thing. You don't want to establish any habits when you're trying to hide.

Calico Jack and his crew captured a larger ship and used it to continue their campaign of terror. With the bigger ship and so much good hunting and good luck, they felt they would never be caught.

Calico Jack and his crew loved to celebrate a good pillaging and the treasure it brought by drinking rum, and lots of it. This never led to clear minds and quick reactions. Instead, the pirates ended up with muddled brains and lazy outlooks.

Around midnight on October 22, 1720, Mary Read and Anne Bonny were on deck, anchored off Point Negril, Jamaica, when they noticed a mysterious sloop glide up alongside them. They recognized it as a sloop belonging to the governor of Jamaica, who had been looking for them.

The women yelled for their shipmates and drew their swords, ready for a fight. It was a futile alarm, though. Everyone else aboard the pirate ship was too drunk to respond, including Calico Jack.

A few pirates roused themselves briefly when the sloop's captain called for immediate surrender. The call to give it up penetrated the captain's stupor and Calico Jack stumbled on deck and began a feeble attempt to resist, but it was no use. The men were in no shape to fight.

The governor's sailors soon overwhelmed the hopelessly drunk pirates, some of whom tried to hide in the ship's hold. It was not a valiant fight to the finish, by any means.

Mary Read and Anne Bonny refused to surrender. They remained on deck and faced the governor's men alone, firing their pistols and swinging their cutlasses. Mary Read became so disgusted with the drunkenness of her fellow pirates that she stopped fighting long enough to peer over the entrance of the hold below and yell, "If there's a man among ye, ye'll come up and fight like the man ye are to be!"

When no responded, she fired a shot down into the hold, killing one of them.

It was over quickly. Calico Jack surrendered, and Mary Read and Anne Bonny and the rest of the crew were overpowered. They were taken prisoner and brought to Jamaica for trial.

Trials did not last long in those days, and in this case, the evidence against these pirates was overwhelming. They had left too many witnesses. On November 16, 1720, they were all found guilty and sentenced to hang.

Anne Bonny was allowed one final visit with Calico Jack before he was hanged. She stayed true to her angry self.

Rather than a gentle and loving and heartfelt goodbye to the man she had sailed with for so long, she entered his cell, looked him up and down, and offered a bit of advice. It probably rang in his ears as he walked up the steps of the gallows the next day.

"If you had fought like a man, you would not be hanged like a dog."

Anne Bonny and Mary Read were tried a week later, found guilty, and sentenced to be hanged.

However, they each got a temporary reprieve. They were both pregnant, and because the British law that ruled Jamaica forbid hanging pregnant women, they were sent to jail until the babies were born.

The fearsome reign of the female pirates was over. They had defied the odds and fought with passion and bravery until the end.

There is some mystery and confusion about what happened after the trials of Mary Read and Anne Bonny. One account says it was not a happy ending for Mary Read, because she died from fever the next year, still in jail. Another story says she faked her death and was smuggled from prison, living the rest of her life quietly and peacefully.

There is no record of Anne Bonny's execution. Some say that her wealthy father paid a ransom for her release. Afterward, the story goes, she moved to an unnamed island, had her child, and opened a tavern, entertaining her guests with stories of her pirate days.

Another tale says that both women moved to Louisiana, where they raised their children and were friends for the rest of their lives. It's a mystery waiting to be solved.

OTHER FAMOUS WOMEN WHO DISGUISED THEMSELVES AS MEN

- Rena Kanokogi disguises herself as a man to enter a judo tournament in 1959. She wins, but loses her title when it is discovered she is a woman. That doesn't stop her—she continues to fight for her dreams, and becomes the world's first female judo world champion.

- Sarah Edmonds serves as a member of the Union army, as a field nurse and a spy—and as a man.

- Hua Mulan takes her father's place in the Chinese army. She may exist more in the realm of legend than real life, as her story is thought to have originated from a potentially fictional ballad.

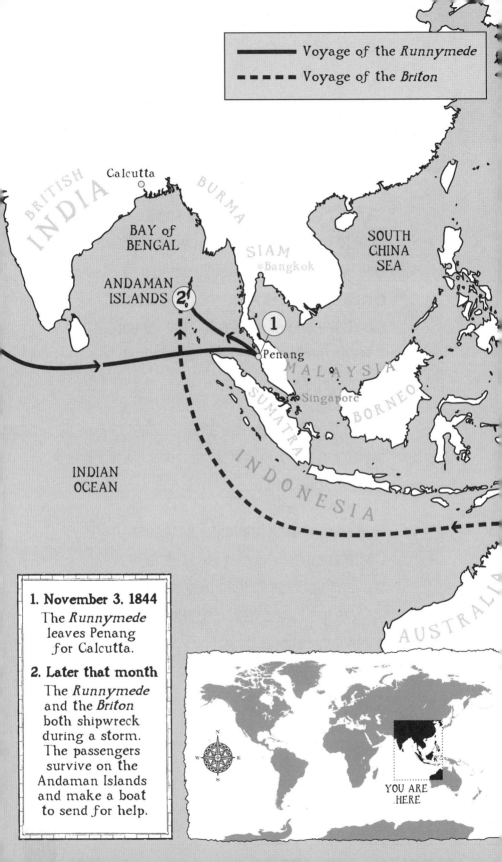

Voyage of the *Runnymede*

Voyage of the *Briton*

Calcutta

BRITISH INDIA

BURMA

BAY of BENGAL

SIAM

⊙Bangkok

SOUTH CHINA SEA

ANDAMAN ISLANDS ②

①

○Penang

MALAYSIA

⊙Singapore

BORNEO

SUMATRA

INDONESIA

INDIAN OCEAN

AUSTRALIA

1. November 3, 1844

The *Runnymede* leaves Penang for Calcutta.

2. Later that month

The *Runnymede* and the *Briton* both shipwreck during a storm. The passengers survive on the Andaman Islands and make a boat to send for help.

N
W E
S

YOU ARE HERE

Chapter Four

The Wild Men of the Andamans

Captain William Clement Doutty was more
nervous than usual as he sat aboard his
ship, the *Runnymede,* still tied to the dock
at Graves End in the warm English sun.
He could not shake his bad feelings about
his next voyage and it bothered him as the
Runnymede rocked gently against the pier.

It was Captain Doutty's job to be nervous before
he set sail. There were many details to take care
of and many people depending on him. But this
time, the feeling stayed with him, woke him in
the middle of the night, and invaded his stomach
to the point he could not eat. This trip, he thought
to himself, will be the hardest I have ever made.

Three things bothered him. The first was his
cargo. Instead of barrels of coffee and bales of

cotton and wool, he was transporting English soldiers and their families. More than 300 people would make this trip on the *Runnymede*, moving to India to serve the Queen. Human cargo was always more unpredictable than bales of cotton. The long voyage would be a test for people who were not used to being at sea.

The second challenge was the Bay of Bengal, which he would have to sail through on the final approach to Calcutta. The Bay of Bengal is a place of sudden, unpredictable hurricanes. These storms are so powerful that they have erased entire islands from the map.

On that last part of the trip, Captain Doutty would have to sail with his fingers crossed and hope the *Runnymede* would be safe.

The third challenge that woke him from deep sleep was worse than the other two combined. To get to Calcutta, the *Runnymede* had to pass closely by the Andaman Islands. The stories Captain Doutty had heard about the Andamans sent chills up his spine. Other captains warned him that the people who lived in the Andamans, which the captains called the Wild Men, were not friendly. They captured uninvited guests, killed them, cooked them over a roaring fire, and ate them enthusiastically.

Captain Doutty did not want the troops he was carrying to be someone's dinner. He did not want to be someone's dinner, either.

On June 20, 1844, the *Runnymede* set sail from Graves End, England. Captain Doutty planned well and knew that discipline was the key to a successful journey. He kept the pent-up soldiers active and distracted to keep them out of trouble. He encouraged everyone to come up on deck into the fresh air and fish for sharks or shoot birds flying by as they headed south. He set up checker boards and other games to play. He encouraged everyone to read the many books on board. Captain Doutty made the schedule as regular as it could be, serving dinner each day at 4 in the afternoon.

Things began to go sour only two weeks into the voyage. William Bryant, a private in Her Majesty's 10th Regiment of Foot, soon found it impossible to eat. He found himself at the rail, so seasick that even the water he tried to drink would not stay in his stomach. He died on July 12 and was buried at sea.

William Bryant was the first to go, but not the last. He probably would not have survived what the *Runnymede* went through when it entered the Bay of Bengal four months later, so, in a way, he was lucky.

The *Runnymede* rounded the Cape of Good Hope at the bottom of Africa and headed back north into the Pacific Ocean. For the 300 people living cramped below, it was grueling. They lived in tight quarters below thick pine decks that didn't let in much fresh air. They were dirty and stinky.

Rats and insects crawled over people and blankets and food, making everyone both irritated and sick.

The *Runnymede* made its last stop before Calcutta in the Malaysian Islands. It left Penang at sunrise on the morning of November 3, 1844, with light winds from the south filling its many sails. The *Runnymede* was on the home stretch of its long journey to India, heading into the Bay of Bengal. This part was the most dangerous. Heat and humidity and mixing ocean currents often blended in the Bay of Bengal to a perfect pitch, creating the most powerful storms in the world. Would the *Runnymede* be hit?

Captain Doutty kept his fears to himself. There was no point in alarming his crew or passengers.

By 8 that morning, the weather showed its first sign of unease as the winds picked up. Captain Doutty was on edge. Increasing winds were never a good sign. He ordered his sailors to drop the mainsail. By 10, the captain knew there was trouble ahead. The smaller sails at the top of the mainmast had been torn to shreds and sent in rags to the sea below by the raging wind.

By midday, darkening clouds blocked out the bright tropical sun. There was nothing to do but wait out the roaring winds. There were no maneuvers to try in the middle of a hurricane. The experienced captain could only try to use the ship's rudder to keep the *Runnymede* pointed in the right direction. Seasoned seamen knew one had to simply ride it out and hope for the best.

An explosion of wind blew the last sail away. The *Runnymede* was at the mercy of the storm. Lifeboats were ripped from their stations and tossed into the sea. Hatches were closed tightly to prevent the green ocean water from pouring in below. In the holds, the crew and passengers began to panic. If the ship went down, there would be no escape.

And then came the unrelenting rain.

At 6:30 that evening, the eye of the storm passed over the battered ship and for a just a little while, there was calm. An hour later, the winds returned, stronger than before. The men who had to be on deck could no longer hold onto the rails or anything else and fought to keep from being blown into the sea. Soldiers below began bailing out the water that was pouring in despite the closed hatches. Others manned the pumps, but it was useless. The storm was in control.

The next morning, the *Runnymede* was still being pounded. By then, the three-feet-thick masts were in splinters and the cabins that had once been securely attached to the deck had been ripped off by huge waves, leaving gaping holes.

More than a day into the storm, Captain Doutty noted in his log that the ship became "perfectly unmanageable from her crippled state, but rode all the time like a sea-bird on the waves."

Through the thickness of the storm and the pandemonium, one of the crew spotted another ship ahead, but could not really make it out. Crashing into it would have meant the end of everything and everyone on board both ships— hundreds of people would have quickly sunk to a watery grave. But the mystery ship faded into the storm.

By 8 that night, the hurricane reached its strongest point. Soldiers and crew could no longer stand at the pumps and had to fight the surging water with only buckets. The storm seemed as though it was going to go on forever.

Just as light was slowly growing on the horizon the next day, the worst happened. The *Runnymede*'s rudder was ripped away, lost forever. Losing the rudder meant that whatever weak control Captain Doutty had managed to hold onto was gone.

Hope was fading fast.

Suddenly, the *Runnymede* came to a jarring halt. The ship shook violently, then stopped dead in the water. The ship had struck a coral reef. Everyone on board thought it was the end.

"We felt the ship strike, and gave ourselves up for lost, expecting at any moment to be engulfed in the depths of the ocean," Captain Doutty wrote later.

But that moment never came! In running into the reef, the *Runnymede* was saved. The ship was upright. Everyone was alive. Now they had a chance.

The clouds began to part slowly and, in the distance, Captain Doutty saw surf breaking on a rugged beach ringed by thick mangroves. These gnarly trees with thick roots held the loose sand of the beach in place. It was an island, but what island? He had not been able to check his charts for three days. Without a rudder, the *Runnymede* had drifted at the mercy of the storm. Where were they?

Captain Doutty looked up. The clouds had parted enough that he could see stars in the northwest sky. He checked the stars, then his charts. They were more than 150 miles off course, he figured. His heart sank.

With horror, Captain Doutty realized that they were sitting on a reef that ringed one of the Andaman Islands, home of the Wild Men!

He moved slowly to his cabin, sat on his bunk, and leaned back as he waited for the new day to break. Had they survived the storm only to die an even more horrible death? If the rumors were true, they could be killed and eaten by the Wild Men. Maybe the Wild Men were hiding at that very moment, watching, and waiting.

The *Runnymede* was not expected in India for weeks. No one would be looking for them. He had to get everyone off the ship and onto the beach. Then he had to keep them safe. Was there enough food? How would they live? What would they eat?

Captain Doutty was startled from his thoughts by the sight of one of his men trying to crawl through his cabin window. "We are all alike now," the man cried. "I will no longer obey your orders!" Captain Doutty watched, shocked, as the crazy young man fell into the sea and started swimming for the beach through the turbulent waters. Caught in the surf, unable to push to the surface, he disappeared beneath a wave. When others finally pulled him from the water, he was dead.

The island had claimed its first victim.

Captain Doutty joined the crew back on deck and began to plan. He didn't want to lose any more people.

Sitting on the damp deck of the beached *Runnymede*, members of the crew saw, just 400 yards away, the ship they had spotted during the storm. It was the *Briton*, which had come to rest high on the roots of a large tree in the mangrove swamp. Twelve of the crew lowered themselves to the beach, which was closer than they thought, and walked over to introduce themselves to the crew of the *Briton*.

The *Briton* was larger than the *Runnymede* and had been heading north from Australia to India with a crew, cargo, and more than 300 soldiers,

34 women, and 51 children. Captain Doutty and the *Briton*'s captain now held the lives of more than 600 hungry and frightened survivors in their hands.

Luckily, Captain Doutty was an organizer. The worst had happened and it was time to move ahead. His first duty was getting everyone off the shattered ships and onto the beach. There, in the still and humid air, they could start the work of surviving.

Women and children were guided to the sandy, rocky beach. Anyone able to help was put to work pulling barrels of biscuits from the *Runnymede* and building four large fires. Later, the survivors continued to pull useful things from the ships, such as preserved potatoes, more biscuits, flour, sugar, split peas, and rice. They even brought some soap to shore.

Then it happened. Someone saw what he thought was a group of silent men moving in the trees behind the beach. Another man reported he had heard moaning, a shrill song of some sort that seemed to drift in the air. Was the sound from a pack of animals passing through the jungle?

Or was it something else?

They were all on edge. Captain Doutty knew his job was to distract everyone from dark thoughts of being cooked and eaten. He organized the men and women into teams. He sent one group to find a spring for fresh water. He asked another group to cut out a path through the thick trees for hunting parties. A third group went to the ships to cut down what was left of the sails and build tents. A fourth group scavenged wood for fires.

The most important group was the largest. Captain Doutty chose the strongest men, soldiers who had been in battle and knew how to fight. These men became guards, armed with muskets and swords. They built a shabby defense of trees and boulders and they watched over the new village of frightened survivors.

Captain Doutty had the carpenters from both the *Runnymede* and the *Briton* start building a small, sturdy boat from the scattered wreckage. He needed a boat that could be sent for help.

It was all very hard work. The air was heavy and humid, completely different from the refreshing breezes found on English beaches. Every movement was difficult. But they all wanted to survive and trusted that this was the best way to meet that goal.

One day, a guard saw seven Wild Men emerge from the edge of the jungle. They stared silently at two sailors on the beach who were busy looking for shellfish. Each islander held a long, pointed spear. They quickly surrounded the two sailors and one Wild Man lunged with his spear, but missed. The sailors managed to escape and sped back to the safety of the camp.

Six soldiers from the camp took off in hasty pursuit, but the strange men had disappeared. The soldiers found only a small fire. Scattered around the fire were bones of some kind.

But what kind? Human?

The castaways settled in and explored a bit more each day, always in groups and always armed. They found crabs, prawns, and other shellfish at low tide. They also found the remains of three wrecked ships sitting like skeletons on the beach. What had happened to the people on those ships? Had they died at sea in a storm? Had they survived the storm and met with an uglier fate? No one dared ask.

Captain Doutty had another problem he had not planned on. Like the young man who had jumped into the sea and drowned, some of the survivors did not want to obey orders. It was almost as if the rawness and wildness of the jungle made them a bit wild, too.

Shortly after setting up camp, some of the men attempted to steal a large barrel of ale from a sergeant's tent. They did not seem to care that the ale was guarded by a man with a musket. As they snuck to the tent at night, the guard fired, which sent the robbers into the mangroves, where one of them fell and cried out in great pain.

Captain Doutty moved quickly and firmly to squash any rebellion. The men who had misbehaved were whipped for stealing. Everyone began listening to Captain Doutty.

One morning at the end of the first week, a guard on the beach saw another group of 10 men with spears. They were no more than 200 yards away, staring sullenly at the growing camp. Guards grabbed their muskets and fired three volleys above the islanders' heads to frighten them off. The mysterious men turned and walked calmly into the thick jungle. They did not appear frightened.

Captain Doutty ordered the number of guards doubled at night.

The next day, the Wild Men tried again, launching themselves at the camp, throwing spears at the sentries, and screaming words no one could understand. The guards fired their muskets and the raiders turned and ran back into the jungle. The soldiers began calculating how much ammunition was left.

It seemed clear to Captain Doutty that the Wild Men were looking for weaknesses. It would be only a matter of time before a guard fell asleep or failed to notice a movement in the jungle. When that happened, the Wild Men would attack. At some point, they would win.

On the 25th day after the storm, four soldiers who were hunting for shellfish on the beach crossed an invisible line that only the Wild Men knew about. The Wild Men attacked quickly, throwing their spears and screaming at the soldiers in a way that showed they had done this sort of thing before. This time, the Wild Men were almost successful. One soldier was dragged back to camp with three spears in his back, bleeding intensely and moaning, but still alive.

Captain Doutty ordered an even stronger defense around the camp, with more guards and more muskets.

In a misguided attempt at trapping a Wild Man or two and teaching them a lesson, four soldiers walked down a path into the jungle and left two of their bright red uniform jackets on a mangrove root. They hoped the Wild Men would think it was a peace offering. Then, they slipped silently behind a large tree and waited to ambush anyone who came to take the jackets.

The Wild Men had been watching the entire time and were not impressed with either the jackets or the badly planned ambush. Instead of picking up the jackets, they unleashed nearly 15 sharp spears at the hiding Englishmen, who ran back to camp as fast as they could.

Two things were becoming frighteningly clear to Captain Doutty: The attacks from the Wild Men were coming more often, and, each time, there were more Wild Men involved. How many were there on this tiny island?

Captain Doutty urged the carpenters to hurry with their work on the sailboat. It would be only a matter of time before the Wild Men attacked in full force. Captain Doutty knew that when that attack came, there would be nothing he could do to prevent it.

Near the end of November, the carpenters finally finished the boat, which they christened *Hope*. They had been on the beach for nearly three long and frightening weeks. The entire encampment stood in the shallow waves of the beach and cheered as the *Hope* and its crew of six men pushed off to find help.

The *Hope*, they thought, would make it to the shipping lanes beyond the Andamans and find help. It would take some time and a bit of luck, but the plan might just work. Supplies were running low on the island and, without supplies, it would be hard to survive for long.

Worse, it seemed that the Wild Men were just waiting for the right moment to wipe out the camp and everyone in it.

After the *Hope* left, people settled back into their routines at the encampment. A group of hunters set out from the beach and found and killed an 80-pound wild hog. For the first time in weeks, the survivors had meat!

A number of Wild Men had watched the hog being killed. Three of them managed to surround a soldier and began beating him, ripping off his shirt while he screamed for help. Only the quick actions of the other startled soldiers saved him. One fired into the group of Wild Men. They ran off, leaving their intended victim on the beach, sobbing in relief.

As December began, people were tired, and their motivation and ingenuity had been spent. The nearby beaches had been picked clean of shellfish and ammunition was running low.

To top it off, clouds of mosquitoes began to appear, making any outside activity feel like torture. Enthusiasm and optimism were beginning to fade.

There was no sign of the *Hope.*

Still, Captain Doutty made sure order was maintained. Every Sunday, church services were held in a clearing near the largest group of tents. The gathered congregation prayed to be saved. Soldiers were ordered to dress in their formal uniforms and parade along the beach after the praying and sermons. It must have been an unusual sight to the Wild Men watching curiously from their perches in the mangroves.

On December 15, the entire encampment began to shake so violently everyone streamed from their tents. Earthquake! Luckily, no one was hurt. Perhaps the earthquake was a sign. A guard on a hill behind the camp saw a sail slowly emerging on the horizon.

It was a large ship and it was heading right for them!

Slowly at first, then growing louder, a welcoming murmur became a roar. A sailor ran to the wreck of the *Runnymede* and raised its largest flag on a makeshift mast. Another sailor packed what was left of the gunpowder, quickly tamped it down, and fired the ship's cannon.

Captain Doutty later recalled the moment. "The camp was in great commotion, everyone asking where the sail was, straining their eyes to catch a glimpse of the stranger."

Within an hour, the ship rounded a point of the island and anchored. It was the schooner *George Swinton*, loaded with supplies and food for the long-suffering men, women, and children. Tied to its stern was the *Hope*.

Captain Doutty's plan had worked! The weeks of uncertainty had ended. It would be just a matter of time before they would be off their prison of an island and finally headed for India.

The test was not quite over for one man. In a small boat ferrying a group of survivors to the *Swinton*, he stood, somersaulted into the sea, and disappeared beneath the surface. He drifted to the beach, drowned. He was the last to die.

The night before the last of the joyful survivors were taken aboard the rescue ships, a streaking comet glowed brightly in the sky to the south.

It was an apt ending for an adventure.

> A group of Wild Men watched the rescue from their hiding place, then turned and disappeared. They were probably disappointed to have missed out on a good meal. But they knew there would be other storms, other ships, and other opportunities.

WHAT ELSE IS GOING ON IN 1844?

- The Dominican Republic gains independence from Haiti.

- Samuel Morse, inventor of the Morse Code, sends the first electrical telegram.

- The YMCA is founded in London.

NORTH
SEA

EUROPE

OTTOMAN EMPIRE

BLACK SEA

CASPIAN SEA

SPAIN

ITALY

GREECE

TURKEY

MEDITERRANEAN SEA

○Tlemcen

AFRICA

ARABIA

Early 1500s
Barbarossa
sailed the
Mediterranean Sea,
terrorizing
ships
until his death
in the city
of Tlemcen.

YOU
ARE
HERE

Chapter Five

The Audacious Barbarossa

The short, dark man with the bright-red beard had a plan. Two things would happen if it worked. First, he would become very wealthy. Second, his name would ignite fear in anyone sailing on the vast Mediterranean Sea.

His name was Barbarossa, and he was a daring, skilled, and clever pirate. He was the fiercest anyone had seen in 1504.

His plan was to attack two galleons belonging to Pope Julius II. These large ships were carrying gold and jewels at a leisurely pace across the sea from Genoa to Città Vecchia. The pope was the wealthiest and most powerful man in the lands around the Mediterranean. No one would dare attack his ships. Except, maybe, Barbarossa.

The pope's men were not paying attention to Barbarossa's small boat trailing them in the distance.

The galleons moved smoothly through the sparkling blue water, one behind the other. Each surged ahead as their long wooden oars dug in. The men pulling on the oars were slaves, and there were more than 100 of them. They were chained to their seats below deck and they grunted together as they pulled. It was a sorrowful sound.

The colorful tunics and fine hats of the men on the decks of the two ships let everyone who spotted them know that they were the pope's men. Anyone paying close attention would also know that these ships were carrying a large amount of the pope's treasure.

Barbarossa was certainly paying attention.

He was the kind of guy who planned carefully, and he liked surprising his victims. What he was about to do would spread his fame from the north coast of Africa to the Rock of Gibraltar on the southwestern tip of Europe.

As the pope's galleons moved ahead, the guards relaxed and enjoyed the beautiful Mediterranean weather. The sun was warm and pleasant. The sea was calm. Barbarossa and his ship crept closer.

Not a single one of the pope's guards bothered to look back.

Barbarossa was so skillful at reading the wind that he caught a final gust, dropped his mainsail, and coasted gently up to the rear of the pope's grand galleon—silently.

About three seconds later, noise erupted, and a lot of it. Barbarossa and his men leaped to the main deck of the pope's ship, screaming insults at the guards, their sharp swords whirring in the air like lethal hornets.

The guards jumped with alarm. But it was too late. Barbarossa had caught them by surprise. The guards stood with their mouths wide open, unable to move. What in the world was going on? Who was this man with the red beard? Barbarossa and his crew quickly tied them up, stole the guards' colorful uniforms, and put them on.

Now, from a distance, Barbarossa and his motley crew of pirates looked like the pope's guard.

Barbarossa had his men row the captured galleon up to the pope's other galleon, which was moving ahead. No one on the lead ship had noticed the skirmish that had just happened behind them. The lead ship always carried the chests full of gold and the barrels of sapphires, rubies, and diamonds. The men on board looked back at the approaching ship and thought their friends wanted to talk. They ordered the slaves below to stop rowing. Maybe we can take a short break, they thought.

This was exactly what Barbarossa wanted them to think. When the two ships met, Barbarossa and his crew attacked quickly for a second time, flashing their swords and cursing, knocking guards to the deck and kicking them as they lay there.

It was only a matter of minutes before the ship and all its treasure belonged to Barbarossa.

Barbarossa went below the decks of the two ships and unchained every slave. At first, the stunned slaves were not sure why the man with the red beard was cutting off the chains around their ankles. They began to smile, just a little bit.

Barbarossa ordered his men to take the pope's guards below the decks and chain them to the damp seats. A few cried as the rusty chains were strapped to their ankles.

"Row," Barbarossa ordered.

And so they rowed. Sitting where only a short time before the slaves had labored so hard, the pope's men were getting a taste of their own medicine.

When the freed slaves realized what was happening, they let out a wild cheer. Every one of them decided at that moment that they'd sail to the ends of the earth for Barbarossa.

This is not to say that Barbarossa was a kind man. He could be brutal and mean. Being a pirate is a nasty business that involves guns, explosions, and often death. But he wasn't completely missing a heart.

When the pope heard the news that his galleons had been stolen and his guards turned into slaves, he grew very angry. He ordered his navy to find the red-bearded man. And when you do, the pope said, capture him and kill him.

How did Barbarossa come to make such a bad impression on the wealthiest and most powerful man in the Mediterranean? How exactly does anyone become a great and clever pirate?

If you study Barbarossa's life, you might think his path toward piracy was practically an accident.

Barbarossa's father was a potter on the Greek island of Lesbos, a charming and friendly place where everyone knew each other. His bowls, plates, pitchers, and cups were beautiful, useful, and popular on Lesbos. But there were not enough people on Lesbos to support his business. Barbarossa's father wanted to expand his pottery business to neighboring islands.

He bought a boat. One morning, he gathered his three sons on a sunny beach to teach them about sailing. He taught them how to read the sky and the clouds, and how to anticipate bad weather that could sink boats in an instant.

He told them of the many winds of the Mediterranean that were so strong and unpredictable that sailors had named them and were wary of them. There was the *sirocco* that came out of the hot deserts of Africa to the south. There was the *mistral*, which shot down from the mountain valleys of Europe to the north. When these winds arrived, ships would sink and crews would drown if sailors were caught unprepared.

The brothers learned about currents, tides, and how to use a sail to go faster than anyone.

They were experts when they finished their father's lessons. Of the three brothers, Barbarossa was the quickest learner. He'll be a famous sailor one day, the father thought.

On his first trip away from Lesbos to sell his father's pottery on the island of Samos, Barbarossa noticed a merchant ship filled with fine cloth and gold and silver on its way to market. It was packed full of wonderful goods.

On his second trip, Barbarossa saw three other merchant ships, each overflowing with wondrous things to sell. He noticed the difference between his ship and those ships. He could sail to three islands with his father's pottery and return to Lesbos with only 40 drachmas, barely enough to buy food for the family.

Those merchant ships must be worth far more than his father's pottery.

Soon after, Barbarossa used his sailing skills to raid his first ship. He tried what would become his trademark—surprise. Attacking when no one thought he would, he stole everything in the unsuspecting merchant's deep holds. Then he sold it on Paros, a nearby island, and made more money than his father made in an entire year.

Soon, Barbarossa would raid the pope's galleons and became famous. He went on to capture so many ships and steal so much gold and silver that he soon had his own pirate navy. With money from the capture of the pope's galleons, Barbarossa set up a base in North Africa, on what was called the Barbary Coast.

Barbarossa was very smart and always looked for ways to improve his skills. He captured so many ships from different countries and took so many prisoners that he learned to speak five languages.

Barbarossa worked very hard. At first he was very careful, planning each of his attacks so nothing went wrong. He captured some ships and burned others. With each ship, he got richer.

And he was not shy about slicing off arms or ears or legs to get what he wanted.

For the next 14 years, Barbarossa plundered, raided, and grew very wealthy though his violent efforts around the Mediterranean Sea. Barbarossa had a reputation for fierceness that few others matched, and his enemies stretched across the kingdoms of Europe. Many rulers wanted his head! The pope certainly did, and so did the king of Spain.

So did other kings and princes who had lost ships, crews, and money to the red-bearded man. His victims became so angry at Barbarossa and other pirates that they formed a group called the Knights of Malta to find him. These knights would cause a problem for Barbarossa later on.

Barbarossa continued attacking when no one thought it was possible. He loved surprise and was very good at it.

Once, he snuck up on a Spanish ship during a violent storm. Sails had been torn from the masts, making the ship impossible to steer. The sailors and officers were either down below the decks, so seasick they could hardly move, or up by the rails outside, gasping for fresh air. The Spanish sailors were miserable and praying to be saved.

Barbarossa knew it was the perfect time to attack. He caught the ship, jumped on board with his men, and took control. The Spaniards were so weak and seasick they could only watch. They had no energy to fight.

Soon after, Barbarossa made his first mistake.

He attacked a ship carrying the Knights of Malta. Barbarossa and his men snuck up on the ship on a starless night. When he jumped on deck, Barbarossa ordered his crew to throw all the oars into the water. The ship was powerless, able to only coast along in the current.

Barbarossa and his men ransacked the ship, taking what they wanted and tossing the rest into the dark sea. Then, they climbed back onto their own ship and rowed off, leaving the knights adrift. The Knights of Malta stood on the ship's deck and watched as Barbarossa slipped away.

It was not a good idea to make the Knights of Malta angry.

Still, Barbarossa expanded his grip over the Mediterranean, from Turkey in the east, across the port cities of North Africa, and all the way west to Spain and France. Many people wondered what would happen to Barbarossa if he was caught. People wondered if he would make a mistake.

Sometimes, the best planning and the cleverest plans go wrong.

Barbarossa and his older brother learned this in a very difficult way. They attacked another ship carrying the Knights of Malta, who had been looking for Barbarossa ever since he had thrown their oars into the water and left them helpless. The knights had been waiting, and this time were prepared with sharp swords, long and pointed spears, and muskets.

When Barbarossa stepped up on deck, ready to terrorize the crew, he was the surprised one. A knight jumped from behind the mast and swung his sword, hoping to take off Barbarossa's head. Barbarossa ducked and the sword barely missed.

Trying to help, his older brother jumped up, ready to take down the knight who tried to kill his brother. Another knight quickly thrust his spear into the chest of Barbarossa's brother. It ran all the way through, its sharp point emerging from his back as he screamed. He died quickly. Barbarossa and the rest of his men quickly surrendered, for the first time ever.

Barbarossa, his arms and feet tied with leather straps that cut deeply into his skin, was dragged below. He was beaten, insulted, and mocked while the knights carried him in their ship to their castle at Bodrum, in Turkey. The knights spat on him whenever they passed.

For three years, Barbarossa's home was a dark, damp, chilly dungeon deep inside the castle. The knights gave him only scraps of lamb left over from the knights' meals. The dogs had more to eat than Barbarossa. His captors gave him barely enough water to survive and he was constantly thirsty.

Sitting in his small, damp cell, Barbarossa did not see the sun or feel its warmth for the entire three years.

One morning, he woke to screaming and much commotion. He sat up from his bed of dirty straw and listened intently. The noise was not something he normally heard. The knights seemed to be in a panic, screaming at each other for help.

Then Barbarossa heard familiar, comforting voices. It was his younger brother and some of his men! They had been waiting and watching outside the castle for just the right time to surprise the knights and spring Barbarossa free.

After being trapped in a dungeon for three years, many men would have promised to never again to do the things that had gotten them in trouble. They would have hugged their brother, said thank you, and moved back to Lesbos to make pottery.

Not Barbarossa.

His time in prison only made him meaner and fiercer. He was even more popular with his men, who greeted him with cries of joy when he returned to their base. He planned more attacks and quickly grew stronger.

He and his men carried out an attack on a Spanish fort on the North African coast in 1512 that spread Barbarossa's fame more than anything else he had done. The raid polished his reputation for fierceness and courage.

Climbing the high outer wall of the fort, Barbarossa flashed his sword high above his head. A cannon ball fired from inside the fort ripped everything below Barbarossa's elbow off, sending part of his arm flying and leaving only a ragged and bloody stump.

Barbarossa screamed in pain as he clutched what was left of his arm.

Barbarossa was not a man who ever felt sorry for himself. When his wound healed, Barbarossa decided to call attention to what remained of his arm. He ordered a jeweler to make a silver sheath to place over the end of his wound. Soon, he gained a new nickname—"Silver Arm."

As his empire grew, Barbarossa built a gunpowder factory to supply explosives for his many cannons. In 1513, he and his growing group of pirates captured four English ships on their way to France. Then they raided a Spanish city just for the fun of it. To add to the excitement, they later captured four more ships, then moved down the Spanish coast and captured a Spanish galleon.

All the raiding and stealing made the king of Spain angrier than he had ever been. It did not matter how strong Barbarossa had grown, or how much territory he controlled, or how many men fought and raided for him. The king of Spain was far more powerful.

In 1514, Barbarossa and his men captured two more Spanish ships, stole everything, then quickly sailed off to their new hiding spot in North Africa, near the city of Algiers. Later, with 12 ships and 1,000 men under his control, he destroyed two nearby Spanish fortresses.

Business was booming.

By 1516, he and his brother had built a large fortress on the North African coast, and for a short time, Barbarossa turned his attention from the sea to the desert. He wanted to take over a small castle several miles away from the coast, across a sandy expanse of desert.

To get the cannons he needed for the attack, he attached sails to them. He was able to move them easily across the sand, driven by the wind.

Around that time, a sultan invited Barbarossa to his castle for a friendly visit. He told Barbarossa that they should join forces. The sultan thought that his enormous wealth and Barbarossa's skill as a pirate would make a terrific combination. We would be quite a team, the sultan said, as he invited Barbarossa for a stay. The sultan did not understand Barbarossa's thirst for power and what he would do to get it.

Barbarossa agreed to visit. He and the sultan sat together at a grand feast and talked of their plans. Barbarossa's plans, however, did not include the sultan. That night, while the sultan was relaxing in his bath, Barbarossa snuck up and slit the man's throat from ear to ear.

Even with one arm, Barbarossa was very effective with a knife.

He had spread himself too thinly, though. He controlled a lot of land in North Africa, but he did not have enough men to help him defend it. Barbarossa had a long list of enemies, and he had picked the wrong time to fight Spain and its king. Spain had become the most powerful country in the world.

And Barbarossa had made a terrible mistake. The king of Spain wanted the same land in North Africa that Barbarossa wanted.

In May 1518, an army of 10,000 Spanish soldiers—far more men than Barbarossa had—marched to the city of Tlemcen. Barbarossa planned to defend the city, but he had a much smaller group of about 1,000 men.

These were not good odds. There was also the fact that Barbarossa, a man incredibly skilled with ships at sea, was stuck in a fort, on land. He had no sails or ships or skills that would help him win the battle.

He did have courage. And so did his men. On land or sea, they were not about to surrender easily to the Spanish army. In fact, they were not about to surrender at all.

Barbarossa and his men fought without stopping for 20 days. It was an admirable feat. But a vast sea of Spanish soldiers kept coming. Barbarossa's men fought to the last drop of blood.

> Barbarossa was with his men every step of the way. When the end came, he went out like a madman. With his one arm, he swung his sword at the Spanish attackers as they came at him, one after the other, until a cannon ball knocked him from his feet.
>
> When he fell, a dozen Spaniards, swords drawn, quickly pounced on him. In an instant, Barbarossa was dead. A Spanish soldier recalled the moment later: "He fought with his one arm like a lion to the last."

WHAT ELSE IS GOING ON IN 1504?

- That year was a leap year. Although 512 years have passed between 1504 and 2016, there have been only 126 leap years.

- Michelangelo's famous sculpture of David is displayed in Florence, Italy.

- Leonardo da Vinci, credited with inventing everything from paleontology to the parachute, is in the middle of painting the *Mona Lisa*.

ambitious: to wish for achievement or distinction, such as power, honor, fame, or wealth.

ambush: a surprise attack.

anticipate: to expect or predict.

apoplexy: a period of unconsciousness due to a stroke.

audacious: showing a willingness to take surprisingly bold risks.

barracks: housing for soldiers.

barren: bare land with poor soil and few plants.

burly: large and strong.

cairn: a mound of stones piled on top of each other as a marker.

cannibal: an animal that eats its own species.

cargo: goods or materials that are carried or transported by a vehicle.

castaway: a person who has been shipwrecked and stranded in an isolated place.

commission: a directive or assignment of an officer in the military.

composure: a feeling of calm and being in control.

consume: to eat or drink or use up a resource.

crest: an emblem or design used to represent a family or group.

cutlass: a short sword with a slightly curved blade.

desolate: an empty place with no people.

disgruntled: angry or dissatisfied.

eloquent: using language clearly and effectively, showing feeling and meaning.

elusive: difficult to find, catch, or achieve.

endeavor: an attempt to achieve a goal.

excursion: a short journey or trip.

executioner: an official who carries out a sentence of death on a legally condemned person.

exhume: to dig something up from the ground.

expedition: a trip taken by a group of people for a specific purpose, such as exploration, scientific research, or war.

fabled: mythical, imaginary.

fatal: causing death.

fate: the development of events beyond a person's control.

feat: an achievement that requires great courage, skill, or strength.

flabbergasted: astonished.

flimsy: easily damaged.

floes: large, flat pieces of sea ice.

flog: to beat with a whip or stick as punishment or torture.

frenzy: uncontrolled excitement or wild behavior.

futile: pointless.

galleon: a sailing ship used before the eighteenth century.

grueling: extremely tiring and demanding.

ignorant: uneducated or awareness about something.

industry: the large-scale production of something.

infamous: well known for some bad quality or deed.

ingenuity: the ability to solve difficult problems creatively.

knell: the sound of a bell, especially when rung solemnly for a death or funeral.

leeward side: the side that doesn't get hit by the traveling winds.

leisurely: unhurried or relaxed.

lethal: harmful or destructive, causing death.

machete: a broad, heavy knife used as a weapon.

makeshift: a temporary substitute or device.

malicious: intending to do harm.

mangrove: a tree or shrub that grows in tropical coastal swamps.

massacre: the deliberate killing of many people.

melancholy: feeling or making someone feel a thoughtful sadness.

menacing: threatening.

motivation: the reason someone has for behaving a certain way.

motley: assorted or varied.

muddled: confusing, disordered.

musket: an infantryman's light gun with a long barrel, fired from the shoulder.

mutilate: to inflict serious damage on.

noose: a loop with a running knot that tightens as the rope or wire is pulled.

optimism: hopefulness and confidence about the future.

pandemonium: wild and noisy confusion.

pelt: an animal skin.

pillage: to rob and steal during wartime.

plaque: an ornamental in honor of a person or event.

plunder: to steal in a time of war or civil disorder.

predicament: a difficult, unpleasant, or embarrassing situation.

prolong: to extend the duration of something.

promotion: raising someone to a higher position or rank.

provision: food, drink, or equipment for a long journey.

pummel: to strike repeatedly, typically with the fists.

ransack: to go hurriedly through a place stealing things and causing damage.

reef: a ridge of jagged rock, coral, or sand just above or below the surface of the sea.

reputation: the beliefs or opinions that are generally held about someone or something.

rudder: a flat piece of wood, metal, or plastic, hinged vertically near the stern of a boat or ship for steering.

salvation: to be saved.

scabbard: a sheath that holds a sword.

schooner: a type of sailing ship with two or more masts.

security: safety.

sentimental: a feeling of tenderness, sadness, or nostalgia.

sheath: a protective cover.

skirmish: a brief fight between two groups.

sloop: a one-masted sailboat with a mainsail and a jib.

stupor: a state of near-unconsciousness.

sullen: a sulky or depressed mood.

tendril: something that is thin and curly.

thatched roof: a roof made of dried plant materials such as reeds, straw, and heather.

tunic: a loose shirt made without sleeves worn by men in many ancient cultures.

turbulent: unsteady and violent.

undaunted: not intimidated or discouraged by difficulty, danger, or disappointment.

valiant: courageous and determined.

Mystic Seaport:
mysticseaport.org/learn

After reading this, are you yearning for the sea? Mystic Seaport offers great workshops and camps for kids and adults alike. You could even crew your own tall ship, like the ones mentioned in this book!

Pirate Adventures:
chesapeakepirates.com

Lots of fun pirate activities for kids, curated by an actual pirate crew (kind of)!

Pirate Knots:
thepirateking.com/knots

Work on your sailing knots! These can come in useful in a variety of outdoor activities.

New England Pirate Museum:
piratemuseum.com/ec.html

If you're near Salem, Massachusetts, head to the New England Pirate Museum! No matter where you are in the world, check out their fun, hands-on education curriculum for kids and teachers on their website.

Talk Like a Pirate Day:
September 19

Not the most historically accurate event, but still a fun international day to greet everyone with an "Arrr, matey!"

10/16
1/23